Real Language for Real Life

▲

by Barbara Radin

Hostos Community College of the
City University of New York

Edited by Joan Ashkenas

JAG Publications

To my son Daniel

Published by JAG Publications
11288 Ventura Blvd.
Studio City, CA 91604
(818) 505-9002 telephone and fax

Illustration photographs by Jerry Ward

Design by Words & Deeds

Library of Congress Catalogue Card Number available

Printed in the U.S.A.
10   9   8   7   6   5   4   3   2

Contents

DECISION DRAMAS

Introduction

DECISION DRAMAS: A Way to Promote Communicative Competence in the ESL/Foreign Language Classroom

As an ESL instructor for over fifteen years I have often used dramatic techniques to encourage real language use in the classroom. In my dissertation (Radin, 1987) I showed that these techniques significantly enhance communicative competence and self-esteem when compared to a traditional grammar-based classroom. I find that dramatic techniques can be easily integrated into an ESL curriculum using a technique which I developed with my community college students and call "Decision Dramas".

DECISION DRAMA METHODS AND PROCEDURES

A decision drama revolves around the idea that a conflict exists and a decision must be made. Conflicts may relate to personal, school or societal problems.

PROCEDURES

Students are first asked to preview the topic by asking general questions about it. Next, key vocabulary words are discussed. Then students are given background information about the problem. In some cases this background information may be discussed a day before the drama is scheduled to take place. In other cases, the background information may be discussed right before the drama is to take place. Once the conflict is fully understood and discussed, roles may be chosen. The prime role is that of the person who is to make the decision. The other supporting roles are: family, friends, teachers, advisors, employers, etc. who give advice. Each role-player must understand his/her point of view as well as goal or reason for giving advice or opinion. A few brief notes may be written down by the role-players, but in general all dialogue is to be improvised because in real life we are rarely given an opportunity to rehearse what we are going to say. In addition, each role-player must be able to adjust his register and choice of words to the role being played. This technique thus allows students to practice the socio-linguistic aspects of language use.

In order to ensure maximum participation students should be seated facing each other in a semi-circle. The teacher may sit in the circle as well and help direct the Decision Drama, or once the technique is well-established, may choose a student to direct the action and stand outside the circle.

After each student has offered input and advice (and some students may speak more than once) the decision-maker is asked to leave the room and make the decision. While the student is outside making a decision, the group can discuss what decision they expect the student to reach and why. Sometimes a vote as to how the students think the decision will go can also be taken to heighten the tension. Finally, the student enters and renders the decision and the reasons for it.

Students may be allowed to question their fellow student on his decision making process. He should be able to explain the reasons for coming to the decision as well as the things which influenced the making of the decision. Students thus get personally involved and have a direct stake in the decision being made. Enthusiasm is usually high and the lesson highly communicative.

TEACHER CORRECTION
AND EVALUATION

The teacher should use discretion in how much immediate feed-back to give students. The purpose of the exercise is to improve communication skills, not to influence moral or social attitudes. If students are having trouble in finding words or appropriate phrases the teacher should help so as to move along the communicative process. Grammatical errors might be noted down and discussed after the Decision Drama ends.

CONVERSATION PRACTICE

Conversation practice may be done in groups of two or more. Students should read the conversation together and fill in the missing words. The Key Vocabulary section in each unit contains the words needed to fill in the dialogue. After filling in the dialogue students might try to improvise the dialogue to get further conversation practice.

VOCABULARY PRACTICE

The Vocabulary Practice exercise may be done by students individually or in a group. This exercise helps to reinforce not only vocabulary, but also structures. Students may refer back to the original script to see if their answers are correct.

FOLLOW UP ASSIGNMENTS

Follow up writing assignments may also be given in which students are asked to write on the topics in a variety of ways. Writing assignments include letters, dialogues, narrations, interviews, comparison, contrasts, and research projects. In addition, students might also be asked to bring in their own Decision Dramas.

APPENDIX

Consists of Useful Expressions for Decision Dramas: These offer ways of giving suggestions, rejecting suggestions, expressing agreement or disagreement, thanking and responding to thanks. These will be useful in all of the Decision Dramas.

Dr. Barbara Radin
Hostos Community College

Foreword

The challenging situations in Barbara Radin's Decision Dramas engage students intellectually. Student advice-givers identify with the decision-maker: their roles require a responsible, empathetic attitude. Emotions can run high. In classes of foreign students, native cultural backgrounds will undoubtedly influence heavily. But for all classes, whatever the make-up of students, the controversies pose current and on-going dilemmas for which there is no one correct answer. How fascinating it might be a year from now to get comparisons on the outcomes of these Dramas between one class and another, between one scholastic institution and another, between schools in one part of the country and another!

There is no particular order in which to use these Dramas. Neither is there any order of difficulty. The problems in some stories arise in a high school setting, others in a university or the world of work. In taking their roles, students become aware of the keenness of problems, whether or not those problems might affect their immediate or future lives. The instructor may wish to offer students the opportunity to choose according to their interests. Please note that some Key Vocabulary is found in more than one Drama, for the reason that you may choose a unit toward the end of the book now, and later do one at the beginning, not having used a particular word before. Please note also that all Decision-maker roles, except in Chapters 10, 12 and 19, may be played by either a man or a woman. Simply change the name, i.e., Jan to John, she to he, her to him, etc.

About the illustrations: The art work throughout is very old, mostly from the last century, mostly by anonymous artists. What all have in common is that there is an obvious problem for which someone is giving or taking or seeking advice, with varying degrees of emotion. Some drawings seem to fit the story situation perfectly. Others are less obviously related to the specific subject, but are interesting in themselves. Students may enjoy discussing the drawings and try to imagine what the characters are saying or thinking.

There is really nothing quite like these Decision Dramas. Use them at your discretion: many of them will keep the class involved and talking long after the bell has rung.

Joan Ashkenas, Editor

Stay or go?

DECISION DRAMA 1

PREVIEW

What are your feelings about going back to your native country? When do you plan to go back, if ever? Will you go back only to visit or do you intend to live there someday? Why or why not?

KEY VOCABULARY

training, engineering, potentially, respiratory, advancement, opportunities, match, complicating, factor, fiancee.

BACKGROUND INFORMATION

Robert has just completed his training in engineering at a United States university. Although he has already been offered several jobs in the United States, he must decide whether to stay or go back to his native country.

Robert's parents are getting old. His father has just written him that he is in the hospital with a potentially serious respiratory problem. Except for one cousin, all of Robert's family is in his native country and he misses them very much.

On the other hand, the last time Robert visited his native country he found he had less in common with his old friends. Employment could be found there, but salary and advancement opportunities could not match those in the United States. Another possibly complicating factor is that Robert left a fiancee in his native country, but now, after dating an American girl, he is not sure he really wants to marry his fiancee.

Robert has received several job offers from United States companies, and one offer from a company in his native country. He must decide soon what to do.

POSSIBLE ROLES   Robert, parents, fiancee, aunt and uncle, brothers and sisters, American girlfriend, friends from native country, advisor, representative from American company, representative of company from native country etc.

THE DECISION   Predicted Decision _____

Decision Reached _____

Reason for Decision _____

Exercises

Exercise I: Follow up assignment

Choose one of the following and write a letter or composition.

1. Write a letter from the fiancee to Robert asking him to come back to his native country.

2. Write a formal letter from Robert to either the American company or the native company explaining why he must reject his job offer.

3. Write a composition describing how you felt when you returned to your native country for the first time.

Exercise II: Conversation Practice

In groups of two or more fill in and practice the following conversation. Use the vocabulary from the Key Vocabulary section.

X: What's the matter? You don't look very well.

Y: I'm confused. I've just completed my _____ in _____ and have been offered several jobs.

X: So, what's the problem?

Y: The problem is that my parents are in my native country. They are getting old and my father has a _____ serious _____ problem. They want me to come home and get a job there instead of here in the United States. Another _____ factor is that I have a _____ in my native country.

X: What's wrong with that? You can bring her here and get married here.

Y: It's not that simple. I've been dating an American girl, and now I'm not so sure I want to marry my fiancee!

X: Yes, well I can see now that you really do have problems!

Exercise III: Vocabulary Practice

Fill in the blanks with the appropriate words.

Robert has just _____ his training in engineering at a United States _____. Although he has already been _____ several jobs in the United States, he must _____ whether to _____ in the United States or go _____ to his native _____.

Robert's parents are getting _____ and his father has just _____ him that he is in the _____ with a potentially _____ respiratory problem. _____ for one cousin, all of Robert's _____ is in his native country and he _____ them very much.

On the other hand, the _____ time Robert visited his native country he found he had less and less in _____ with his old _____. Employment _____ be found there, but salary and _____ opportunties could not _____ those in the United States. Another possibly _____ factor is that Robert left a _____ in his native _____, but now, after dating an _____ girl he is not sure if he really wants to _____ his fiancee.

Robert has received several job _____ from United States companies, and _____ offer from a company in his native country. He must _____ soon what to do.

Protest a low grade or keep quiet?

DECISION DRAMA 2

PREVIEW

Have you ever received a grade you thought was too low? If so, what did you do about it? Have you ever complained to your teacher about something? What happened? Is the view of the teacher's authority different in your native country than in the United States? Explain.

KEY VOCABULARY

authority, foreign, volunteered, final exam, upset, make it clear, grade change, class participation, head of department, consider, rarely, challenged, complain, observed, protest.

BACKGROUND INFORMATION

Lee is a foreign student who has been in the United States for over a year. He is a freshman in high school. He always got good grades but rarely volunteered or talked in class. In the final exam he got a B+ but received a C+ in the course. Lee is very upset about the grade because he feels that he deserves at least a B. Also, he feels that the teacher didn't make it clear how important class participation was to the final grade.

The problem is whether or not he should complain to the head of the department. The teacher has already said he won't consider a grade change. In Lee's native country the authority of the teacher is rarely challenged. However, in the United States, he has observed several students challenging the teacher's authority. Some other students with a similar problem are planning to complain. They have asked Lee to join them. Lee thinks he may have to take another class with this teacher next year. He must decide whether to protest the low grade or keep quiet.

POSSIBLE ROLES   Lee, teacher, classmates, students planning to complain, parents, school counselor

THE DECISION   Predicted Decision _____

Decision Reached _____

Reason for Decision _____

Exercises

DECISION
DRAMA
2

Exercise I: Follow up assignment:

Choose one of the following.

1. Write about a grade you received that you thought was unfair. Why was it unfair? Did you do anything about it? Why or why not? Tell what happened.

2. Write a dialogue between Lee and the teacher. Then write a dialogue between Lee and the head of the department.

3. Write a composition about the difference between teacher authority in the United States and in your native country. Which system do you prefer and why?

Exercise II: Conversation Practice

In groups of two or more fill in and practice the following conversation. Use the vocabulary words from the Key Vocabulary section.

X: I'm so mad I could cry!

Y: What are you mad about?

X: I'm mad about my final grade. On the _____ I got a B+, but I only got a C+ in the _____.

Y: Did he say why he gave you that grade?

X: He said I rarely _____ or talked in class. I feel he didn't _____ _____ _____ to the class about the importance of _____.

Y: What are you going to do?

X: I've already talked to the teacher and he said that he wouldn't consider a grade change. The next thing I can do is to _____ to the _____.

Y: Do you have the nerve to do it?

X: Well, in my native country the _____ of the teacher is rarely _____. But here I've seen several students _____ the teacher's authority. Some other students are planning to _____ too. Also, I may have to take another class with this teacher later. I have to decide whether to _____ my low grade or just keep quiet.

Exercise III: Vocabulary Practice

Fill in the blanks with the appropriate words.

      Lee is a _____ student who has been in the United States for over a year. He is a freshmen in high school. He always got good _____ but rarely _____ or talked in class. In the _____ exam he got a B+ but received a C+ in the _____. Lee is very _____ about the grade because he feels that he _____ at least a B. Also, Lee feels that the teacher didn't ____ ____ ____ about the importance of class _____ to the final grade.

      The problem is whether or not he should _____ to the _____ of the department. The teacher has already _____ he won't _____ a grade change. In Lee's native country the _____ of the teacher is rarely _____. However, in the United States he has _____ several students challenging the teacher's authority. Some other students with similar complaints are _____ to complain. They have asked Lee to join them. Lee may have to take another _____ with this teacher next year. He must decide whether to _____ the low grade or keep quiet.

Keep quiet or blow the whistle?

DECISION DRAMA 3

PREVIEW

Do you know what a "whistle blower" is? Have you ever been in a situation where you saw someone doing something illegal or immoral? What was your reaction to this?

KEY VOCABULARY

public relations, chemical, raise, promotion, inter-office, illegally dumping, anti-pollution, devices, expose, distressed, financial, campaign, politically active, community-minded, in a good light, conflicted, rash, expose.

BACKGROUND INFORMATION

Rudi is a thirty-five year old single parent working for a chemical company in the public relations department. He has been there for five years and is due to receive a raise and a promotion. He has two children, a son thirteen and daughter nine. He is also politically active and community-minded. Recently, while working late alone in the office he found some inter-office memos which indicated that his company was illegally dumping chemicals into the nearby rivers. He was very distressed and took the information to a close friend in the company. The friend told him that the company was in financial difficulties and couldn't afford anti-pollution devices at this time.

Now Rudi is told he must run a public relations campaign which puts the company in good light. He is conflicted between the need to support his family and get a promotion, or expose what is really going on in his company. A decision must be made soon. What will Rudi do?

POSSIBLE ROLES

Rudi, parents, close friends, boyfriend, children, co-workers.

THE DECISION

Predicted Decision _____

Decision Reached _____

Reason for Decision _____

Exercises

Exercise I: Follow up assignment

Choose one of the following and write a letter or composition.

1. Write a short composition about your feelings about pollution. What are the chief causes of pollution in the world today? What can we do about them?

2. Write a letter from Rudi to the chemical company telling the company why he can no longer work for them.

3. Write a conversation in which Rudi confronts the company officials with illegal dumping.

Exercise II: Conversation Practice

In groups of two or more fill in and practice the following conversation. Use the vocabulary from the Key Vocabulary section.

X: What's the problem? You look worried.

Y: Yes, it's my job. I work in a _____ company in the _____ department. In fact, I'm up for a _____ next month.

X: So, what's the matter?

Y: Well, recently, while working late I found some _____ memos which showed that the company has been _____ chemicals into the nearby rivers.

X: That's not your problem. You don't make company policy. Why can't you pretend that you never saw it?

Y: No, I'm very _____ by the whole thing.

X: Well, I can tell you one thing. The company is probably experiencing _____ difficulties and they can't afford _____ devices at this time.

Y: That might be true, but it still doesn't excuse what they are doing. The worst thing is, now they've asked me to run a public relations _____ to show the company in a good light. I've either got to _____ what they're doing or keep quiet and pretend I don't know anything. But I don't know if I can do that. I've got to be able to live with myself.

X: Remember, you are a single parent with two children to think of. You're due for a _____ soon. Don't do anything rash that you might regret later!

Y: You're right. I'd better think hard before I make this decision.

Exercise III: Vocabulary Practice

Fill the the blanks with the appropriate words.

     Rudi is a thirty-five _____ old single parent working for a _____ company in the public _____ department. He has been working there for five years and is _____ to receive a raise and a _____. He has two children, a son thirteen and a daughter nine. He is also politically _____ and community-minded. Recently _____ working late alone in the _____ he found some inter-office _____ which indicated that his _____ was illegally dumping _____ into the nearby _____. He was very _____ and took the _____ to a close friend in the company. The friend told him that the company was in _____ difficulties and couldn't afford the _____ devices at this time.

     Now Rudi is told that he must run a _____ relations campaign which will put the company in a good _____. He is _____ between the need to _____ his family and get a promotion, or _____ what is really going on in his company. A decision must be made soon.

Get a job, join the army or go to a community college?

DECISION DRAMA 4

PREVIEW

What do you plan to do when you graduate from high school? Do you know anyone who has joined the army? Why did they join? Do you know anyone who has gotten a job after high school? How do they like it? Do you know anyone who has gotten financial aid and gone to a community college?

KEY VOCABULARY

construction business, advancement, impress, career, computers, data processing, financial aid, transfer, urging, army, expenses, room and board, benefits.

BACKGROUND INFORMATION

Andrew has been in the United States for five years and is about to graduate from high school. Although he is fluent in English, he still has trouble with writing. He graduated with a C+ average and now must decide what to do. An uncle in the construction business has offered him a job after graduation. The job is well paid but has few opportunities for advancement. If he takes it, however, he can buy that new car he's been dreaming of and impress his girlfriend.

On the other hand, he's been thinking of a career in computers or data processing. He thinks he might do well going to the community college in his neighborhood. He could get financial aid and work part time to pay expenses. If he does well he could transfer to a four-year college.

Finally, some of his friends are urging him to join the army. There he could have free room and board, good pay and benefits and he could learn a skill such as computer science, as well. They say it's a free way to see the world. Andrew must decide what to do: work with his uncle, join the army or go to a community college.

POSSIBLE ROLES   Andrew, parents, friends, data processors, uncle who owns a construction company, co-worker in the company, army recruiters, college counselor.

THE DECISION   Predicted Decision _____

Decision Reached _____

Reason for Decision _____

Exercises

Exercise I: Follow up assignment

Choose one of the following.

1. Write a composition on what career you plan to choose. Why? How many years of college will you need?

2. Write a conversation between two people discussing the advantages or disadvantages of joining the army. Or tell about the experience of someone you know who has joined the army.

3. Find out what forms of financial aid are available to students who want to go to college. Write a composition.

Exercise II: Conversation Practice

In groups of two or more fill in and practice the following conversation. Use the vocabulary from the Key Vocabulary section.

X: What are you thinking about?

Y: I'm thinking about my future.

X: What are you going to do?

Y: I'm not sure. I have an uncle in the _____ _____ who'll give me a job. The job pays well but there are few opportunities for _____.

    On the other hand, I could buy the car I've been dreaming of and _____ my girlfriend.

Y: So, what's the problem?

X: I'm not sure that's what I want. I've also been thinking of a _____ in _____ or ____ _____. I've only got a C+ _____ but I could go to community college. I could work _____ to pay _____ and then maybe _____ to a four-year college.

Y: That sounds like a good idea.

X: Yes, it does. But to complicate things even further, some of my friends have been urging me to join the _____. They say I'll get free ____ and _____, good pay and good benefits and I could learn a skill such as computer science as well. They also say it's a free way to see the _____. I'm really confused!

Y: Well, good luck with your decision. Let me know which path you choose.

Exercise III: Vocabulary Practice

Fill in the blanks with the appropriate words.

Andrew has _____ in the United States for five years and is about to _____ from high school. Although he is _____ in English he still has some trouble with writing. He graduated with a C+ _____ and now must decide what to do. An uncle in the _____ business has _____ him a job after graduation. The job is well paid but has ____ opportunites for advancement. If he takes it, however, he can buy that new car he's been dreaming of and _____ his girlfriend.

On the other hand, he's been thinking of a _____ in computers or data _____. He thinks he might do well going to the community college in his _____. He could get _____ aid and also work part-time to pay expenses. If he does well he could _____ to a four-year college. Finally, some of his friends are _____ him to _____ the army. There he could have free room and _____, good pay and _____ and he could learn a skill such as computer science as well. They say it's a free way to see the _____. Andrew must decide what to do: work with his _____, join the _____ or go to a _____ _____.

Bilingual program or immersion?

DECISION DRAMA 5

PREVIEW

What do you think of bilingual education? Have you ever been in a bilingual program or known someone who was? Do you think it is a successful way to learn a language? What is an immersion program? Have you ever been in one? Do you think this is a good way to learn a language?

KEY VOCABULARY

bilingual program, immersion program, relate to, intensively, rapidly, special.

BACKGROUND INFORMATION

Eva came to the United States six months ago. She has a son who will begin high school next year. She would like him to learn English as quickly as possible. He was placed in a bilingual program in his junior high school. There he takes classes in English as a Second Language (ESL). His subject classes are given in his native language. The Bilingual Program Director has explained to her that as he learns more English he will take more of his subject matter in English. He is happy in this program because he has many friends and he is doing well. However, he still speaks mostly his native language because his friends and family speak it. Next year he has a choice of going to the local high school which has an excellent bilingual program, or to a small magnet school which offers a special English immersion program. In the magnet school, he would learn English quickly and then go on to take all his subjects in English. Most of his friends, however, are going to the local high school, and he would like to be with them. Eva must decide what to do: send her son to the high school with the bilingual program or send him to the magnet school with an English immersion program. She must make application soon.

POSSIBLE ROLES   Eva, her son, his friends, his teacher, the Bilingual Program Director, the Immersion Program Director, family members, other parents.

THE DECISION   Predicted Decision _____

                       Decision Reached _____

                       Reason for Decision _____

Exercises

Exercise I: Follow up assignment

Choose one of the following.

1. Tell about your experiences in either a bilingual or an immersion program.

2. Write on the advantages and disadvantages of bilingual education.

3. Investigate immersion programs. Countries like Canada and Israel use these programs to teach language. Are they effective? Why?

Exercise II: Conversation Practice

In groups of two or more fill in and practice the following conversation. Use the vocabulary from the Key Vocabulary section.

X: I have a problem. My son is finishing junior high school this year. Now he's in a _____ where he takes _____ and also takes some of his subjects in his native language. Next year I have to decide whether to send him to the _____ high school which has an excellent bilingual program or to a small _____ school where they have a special _____ program.

Y: What kind of a program is that?

X: It's a program where the students learn English _____. After that he would take all his subjects in English.

Y: You mean he would learn English more _____?

X: Yes, I think so.

Y: So, what's the problem?

X: The problem is that most of his friends have decided to go to the local high school with the bilingual program. He enjoys being with his friends. The trouble is that they all speak his language and he's not learning enough English. I just don't know what to do!

Exercise III: Vocabulary Practice

Fill in the blanks with the appropriate words.

Eva _____ to the United States six _____ ago. She has a son who will _____ high school

next year. She would like him to _____ English as quickly as possible. He is in a bilingual _____ in

junior high school. There he takes classes in _____ as a Second Language (ESL). His _____ classes

are given in his native _____. The Bilingual Program Director has _____ to her that as he

learns _____ English he will take more of his subject matter in English. He is _____ in this program

because he has many friends and he is _____ well. However, he still speaks _____ his native language

because all his friends and family speak it. Next year he has a ____ of going to the _____ high school

which has an _____ bilingual program or to a small _____ school which offers a special English

_____ program. In the magnet school he _____ learn English quickly and then go on to take all

his _____ in English. Most of his friends, however, have _____ to go to the _____ high

school, and he would like to be with them. Eva _____ decide what to do: _____ her son to the high

school with the bilingual program or send him to the magnet school with an English immersion

program. She must make a _____ soon.

Major in the liberal arts or study for a career?

DECISION DRAMA 6

PREVIEW

Which do you think is better: to have a broad based liberal education or to study for a specific career? Why do you think so?

KEY VOCABULARY

career, sophomore, confused, political science, literature, sociology, major in, liberal arts, prefer, specialized, narrowly, skill, computer science, outdated, salary, philosophy.

BACKGROUND INFORMATION

Michael is entering his sophomore year of college and he is confused. He likes liberal arts subjects like sociology, political science, philosophy and literature. His friends and family all say that he should prepare himself for a career in medicine or law, or go into a computer science or business program. He is not very interested in those subjects. However, he is not sure that majoring in a subject like sociology or literature will lead to a career. His advisor tells him that learning to think is more important than learning a skill. He says that sometimes big companies prefer students with a liberal arts education to those who specialized more narrowly in a career. On the other hand, Michael has known people who studied computer science and came out of college with a job at a good salary. He must make a decision soon. Which will he major in, a liberal arts subject or a career?

POSSIBLE ROLES

Michael, his advisor, his parents, his friends, college graduates, an employer.

THE DECISION   Predicted Decision _____

Decision Reached _____

Reason for Decision _____

Exercises

Exercise I: Follow up assignment

Choose one of the following.

1. Write a composition in which you argue why it is better to major in liberal arts or in a career.

2. Write the dialogue between Michael and his advisor.

3. Write what you think will happen to Michael if he majors in a liberal arts subject?

Exercise II: Conversation Practice

In groups of two or more fill in and practice the following conversation. Use the vocabulary from the Key Vocabulary section.

X: What can I do for you?

Y: I'm a _____ and I'm _____. I like liberal arts subjects like _____, _____,and _____, but my friends and family all say I should be thinking more about a career. They want me to think about a career like _____ or _____or go into business or computer science.

X: Well, you know that many times big _____ prefer students with a _____ background to those who _____ more narrowly in a certain career. Learning how to think can be more important than _____ a skill.

Y: You might be right. However, I have known people who studied practical subjects like _____ _____ and come out of college with a good job at a good salary, while those who studied liberal arts had a hard time finding anything at all.

X: Well, it's entirely up to you. Do what you feel is best for you. Let me know what you decide.

Exercise III: Vocabulary Practice
Fill in the blanks with the appropriate words.

Michael is entering his _____ year of college and he is confused. He likes liberal _____ subjects like sociology, psychology and literature, but his friends and family all say that he should start thinking about a _____ like medicine or go into a computer science or business program. He is not _____ that majoring in a subject like sociology or literature will _____ to a career. His advisor has told him that sometimes big companies _____ students with a liberal arts education to those who specialized more _____ in a career. Learning how to think can be more _____ than learning a _____. On the other hand, he has known people who studied computer sciences come out of college with a job at a good _____. He must make a _____ soon. Which will he _____ in, the liberal arts or a career?

Extended family: Live together or live separately?

DECISION DRAMA 7

PREVIEW

What do you think of living together with your mother/father, relatives after you get married? Does this happen often in your native country? How do Americans usually feel about it? Where do old people live in your country? Where do they live in the United States?

KEY VOCABULARY

foreign, economics, engaged, widowed, permanently, common, extended, separately, put her foot down, living together, risk, hurting.

BACKGROUND INFORMATION

Kim is a foreign student in economics. He is engaged to an American girl and plans to be married next month. He has just received a letter from his widowed mother saying that when she comes to the wedding she would like to stay permanently with Kim and his new wife. She says she misses her only son. She feels old and alone and would like to be with him. In Kim's native country it is quite common for a mother to live with her children, especially if they are married. She could help them with the expenses and help take care of the grandchildren. Kim's fiancee, however, being American, is used to parents living separately from their children. She doesn't mind if his mother wants to visit them for a few weeks or a month, but has put her foot down when it comes to living together permanently.

Kim must decide what to do. Should he tell his mother the truth and risk hurting her, or should he invite her to come live with them and risk losing his fiancee? He must make a decision soon.

POSSIBLE ROLES   Kim, his fiancee, his mother, his friends from his native country, his American friends, his relatives, school advisor.

THE DECISION   Predicted Decision _____

Decision Reached _____

Reason for Decision _____

Exercises

Exercise I: Follow up assignment

Choose one of the following.

1. Tell about an experience you had when a relative came to live with you and your family.

2. Compare and contrast American customs about family members living together and customs in your native country. How are they similar? How are they different?

3. Interview Americans and ask them how they would feel about living with their husband's/wife's relatives? Ask them why they feel the way they do.

Exercise II: Conversation Practice

In groups of two or more fill in and practice the following conversation. Use the vocabulary words from the Key Vocabulary section.

X: Can I help you?

Y: Yes, Counselor, I need some advice. I am a _____student and I'm studying_____here at the University. I just received a letter from my_____mother and I'm very worried.

X: Is there anything wrong with your mother?

Y: No, not really. She's coming here for my wedding next _____. The only problem is that she would like to stay permanently with me and my new wife.

X: So what's wrong with that?

Y: Well, you see, she feels old and alone. She_____me and wants to be with me. In my country it is quite common for a mother to live with her married children. She could help them with the_____and help____ _____ of the grandchildren. But my fiancee is American.

X: I see. Well, then you do have a problem. Most Americans are used to parents living_____from their children.

Y: Yes, my fiancee doesn't mind if she wants to visit for a few weeks or months, but she has put her _____ down when it comes to_____ ____ permanently. I don't know what to do. If I tell her the truth I_____hurting her. But if I let her come live with me I risk losing my fiancee!

X: I wish I could help you, but I think that's a decision only you can make.

Exercise III: Vocabulary Practice

Fill in the blanks with the appropriate words.

Kim is a foreign student in economics. He is_____to an American girl and plans to be married next month. He has just received a letter from his_____mother saying that when she comes to the _____ she would like to stay permanently with Kim and his new wife. She says she_____her only son. She feels old and_____and would like to be with him. In Kim's native country it is quite_____for a mother to live with her children, especially if they are married. She could help them with the expenses and help take care of the _____. Kim's fiancee, however, being American, is used to parents living_____from their children. She doesn't mind if his mother wants to_____them for a few weeks or a month, but she has ____ ____ ____ ____ when it comes to living together.

Kim must decide what to do. Should he tell his mother the truth and risk hurting her, or should he invite her to come live with them and risk _____ his_____? He must make a decision soon.

High School: Drop out or stay in?

DECISION DRAMA 8

PREVIEW

Do you know any high school drop outs? Is there a drop out problem in your native country? How is the problem similar or different here?

KEY VOCABULARY

drop out, cutting class, boring, hanging out, rarely, excessive absences, GED.

BACKGROUND INFORMATION

Elizabeth is a junior in a public high school. She is generally an average student. She is doing well in some subjects but failing others. She is not very interested in studying, and doesn't know what she wants to do. For the past six months she has been cutting classes with a group of friends who find school boring and "a drag". Recently she has been cutting whole days and even weeks of school. Elizabeth and her friends have been hanging out and going to various places around the city. Although some of her friends smoke, drink and take drugs, she does this only rarely.

Elizabeth's parents both work and were not aware of the problem until they received a letter from the school informing them about excessive absences. They are very upset and want their daughter to go back to school immediately and stop seeing her friends. Her parents tell her she will never get a good job without a high school diploma. However, she doesn't want to give up her friends and their way of life. Some of them have already dropped out of school and want her to do the same. They say she could get a job or get a GED at 18 and go to a community college. A few friends have gone back to school. Elizabeth must decide what to do: drop out or stay in school.

POSSIBLE ROLES   Elizabeth, parents, brothers, sisters, friends who dropped out, friend who went back to school, girlfriend/boyfriend, teacher, guidance counselor.

THE DECISION   Predicted Decision _____

Decision Reached _____

Reason for Decision _____

Exercises

Exercise I: Follow up assignment

Choose one of the following.

1. Write a composition about why so many young people are dropping out of high school today. What can be done about this situation?

2. Write a letter to a friend about a person you know who has dropped out of high school and what happened to him/her?

3. Compare the problem of high school drop outs in your native country with the problem in the United States. What are the similarities? differences?

Exercise II: Conversation Practice

In groups of two or more fill in and practice the following conversation. Use the vocabulary from the Key Vocabulary section.

X: What's the matter? You look troubled.

Y: I don't know what to do. I think I might _____ _____ of high school.

X: How are you doing in school?

Y: I'm passing some courses and _____ some others. But the real problem is that I've been _____ _____ with some friends.

X: Why do you do it?

Y: Well, we find school _____. My friends and I find school a _____ at times.

X: What do you do when you cut?

Y: We just ____ _____ and go to _____ places around the city. Some of the kids smoke and drink, but I don't.

X: What do your parents think?

Y: Well, they didn't know about it until they received a letter from the school informing them about my ____ _____. Now they are very _____ and want me to go back to school immediately. They also want me to stop seeing my friends.

X: What do your friends think?

Y: They are _____ me to drop out and maybe get a job or get a _____ and then go to a _____ _____.

X: Well, you've got a hard choice to make. I hope you make the right decision!

Exercise III: Vocabulary Practice

Fill in the blanks with the appropriate words.

Elizabeth is a junior in a public high school. She is generally an _____ student. She is doing

well in some _____ but failing others. For the past six months Elizabeth has been _____ class

with a group of friends who find school _____ and a "drag". Recently she has been cutting whole

days and even weeks of school. Elizabeth and her friends have been _____ _____ and going to

_____ places around the city. Although some of her friends smoke, drink and take _____, she

does this only _____.

Elizabeth's parents both work and were not _____ of the problem until they received a

_____ from the school informing them about the _____ absences. They are very _____ and

want Elizabeth to go back to school immediately and _____ seeing her friends. However, she doesn't

want to give up her friends and their way of _____. Some of her friends have _____ dropped out

of school and want her to do the _____. They say she could get a job or get a GED at 18 and go to a

_____ college. A few friends have already_____back to school. Elizabeth must decide what to

do: drop out or _____ in school.

Drugs: how do you handle them?

DECISION DRAMA 9

PREVIEW

Why is the use of drugs such a problem in our society today? Why do people use drugs? Have you ever used drugs or known anyone who does? What do you think the government should do about drug use?

KEY VOCABULARY

shocked, possessing, juvenile hall, threatened, expulsion, probation, admitted, realize, hanging out, concentration, trust, treatment program, authorities.

BACKGROUND INFORMATION

Frank and his younger brother Joe are the only members of their family in this country. Frank earns enough money to send some home to their parents and to support Joe, who is a junior in high school. Frank was shocked recently when Joe and some of his friends in school were arrested for possessing drugs. Joe spent a night in juvenile hall and was threatened with expulsion from school. Joe admitted to Frank that his best friends and his girlfriend take drugs, and that he did also. He promised to quit and to stay away from anyone who takes drugs. Frank and Joe met with the vice principal of Joe's school, who gave Joe another chance. Joe is now on probation.

Recently, Frank found out that Joe was hanging out with his old friends again. Joe admits now that he takes drugs occasionally. Frank knows that Joe misses classes because he can't get up in time. Frank urges Joe to quit taking drugs and to get into a treatment program, but Joe wants Frank to trust him. He says he can handle it, that he doesn't have a problem.

Joe will soon be eighteen years old. Frank knows that if Joe gets in trouble again he will be treated as an adult and will have a criminal record. Where Frank comes from, people take care of their own problems and don't rely on the authorities. Frank is very worried. He must decide very soon whether to let Joe handle it himself, or to tell him either to get treatment or leave the house.

POSSIBLE ROLES   Frank, Joe, best friends, girlfriend, vice principal, drug treatment counselor, probation officer.

THE DECISION   Predicted Decision _____

Decision Reached _____

Reason for Decision _____

Exercises

Exercise I: Follow up assignment

Choose one of the following.

1. Write a composition on drug use in our society. Why do people use drugs? What can be done to get them to stop?

2. Write about a person you know who has taken drugs or an experience you have had taking drugs.

3. Write a dialogue between Frank and Joe as they discuss Joe's situation.

Exercise II: Conversation Practice

In groups of two or more, fill in and practice the following conversation. Use the vocabulary from the Key Vocabulary section.

X: What's the matter? You look terrible.

Y: I have a problem with my younger brother Joe. He and some friends were _____ at school for _____ drugs. Joe is getting another chance from the vice principal, but he's on _____.

X: Well, I guess he's lucky that that's all.

Y: I'm afraid that's not the end of the story. He really hasn't quit.

X: Why doesn't he get into a _____ treatment program?

Y: I want him to do that, but he keeps saying he doesn't have a problem.

X: What will happen if the _____ officer finds out he's taking drugs again?

Y: That's what worries me. He will be eighteen soon, and he will be treated as an adult.

X: Do you think you can _____ him?

Y: I'm not sure. I have to trust him, or else either tell him to get treatment or leave the house.

X: I know you want to help him. You have a hard decision. Good luck.

Exercise III: Vocabulary Practice

Fill in the blanks with the appropriate words.

Frank and his _____ brother Joe are the only _____ of their family in this country. Frank earns enough money to send some home to their parents and to support Joe, who is a junior in high school. Frank was _____ recently when Joe and some of his friends in school were arrested for _____ drugs. Joe spent a night in _____ hall and was threatened with _____ from school. Joe _____ to Frank that his best friends and his girlfriend take drugs, and that he did also. He promised to _____ and to stay away from anyone who takes drugs. Frank and Joe met with the _____ _____ of Joe's school, who gave Joe another chance. Joe is now on probation.

Recently, Frank found out that Joe was _____ out with his old friends again. Joe _____ now that he takes drugs _____. Frank knows that Joe misses classes because he can't get up in time. Frank _____ Joe to quit taking drugs and to get into a _____ program, but Joe wants Frank to trust him. He says he can _____ it, that he doesn't have a problem.

Joe will soon be eighteen years old. Frank knows that if Joe gets in trouble again he will be _____ as an adult and will have a _____ record. Where Frank comes from, people take care of their own problems and don't rely on the _____. Frank is very worried. He must decide very soon whether to let Joe handle it himself, or to tell him either to get _____ or leave the house.

Divorce or stay married?

DECISION DRAMA 10

PREVIEW

What are your feelings about divorce? Is divorce legal in your country? What causes so much divorce in modern life? Have you been divorced or known anyone who has? How has divorce affected your or their lives?

KEY VOCABULARY

divorce, beautician, nursing, insanely, jealous, accuses, attracted, support, instead of, barely, argue, storming out.

BACKGROUND INFORMATION

Jane is a twenty-eight year old woman who is married but has no children yet. She was a beautician but has gone back to school to study nursing. The problem is that her husband has become insanely jealous when she goes to school and accuses her of being attracted to other men. He doesn't want her to work, but at the same time, he doesn't make enough money to support a family. He feels that instead of becoming a nurse, she should become a mother and stay home with the children. She, too, wants children, but not yet. Now, she really wants to continue her education. She enjoys school, but she has so much homework that she barely has time to cook or clean properly. They argue much of the time, and he has begun storming out of the house and coming home late, his breath smelling of alcohol. She still loves him and he loves her, but she must make a decision: divorce or stay married.

POSSIBLE ROLES

Jane, husband, parents, friends, a marriage counselor.

THE DECISION   Predicted Decision _____

Decision Reached _____

Reason for Decision _____

Exercises

Exercise I: Follow up assignment

Choose one of the following:

1. Write a conversation in which Jane tells her husband that she wants to get divorced.

2. Write a composition on your feelings about divorce.

3. Compare divorce in your country with divorce in the United States. How is it similar? How is it different?

Exercise II : Conversation Practice

In groups of two or more fill in and practice the following conversation. Use the vocabulary from the Key Vocabulary section.

X: I can't take it anymore. He's driving me out of my mind!

Y: What's he doing?

X: Well, you know I used to be a _____. But now I've decided to go back to school to study _____. I want a better life for us and our future children.

Y: So, what's the problem?

X: He is the problem. He's become _____ jealous. When I go to school he always _____ me of being _____ to other men.

Y: What does he want you to do?

X: He wants me to _____ a mother and stay home with the children. But he doesn't really make enough to _____ a family. Besides, I want my children to have more than just the necessities.

Y: Has he become violent?

X: Not really, but recently, he has begun _____ _____ of the house after a fight and coming home late smelling of _____.

Y: Do you still love him?

X: Yes, I still love him and I know he loves me, but is love enough to save my marriage?

Y: I don't know, but you'll have to make a decision soon. You just can't go on like this.

Exercise III: Vocabulary Practice

Fill in the blanks with the appropriate words.

Jane is a twenty-eight year old woman who is married but has no children yet. She was a

_____ but has gone back to school to _____ nursing. The problem is that her husband has

become _____ jealous when she goes to school and always accuses her of being _____ to other men.

He feels that ____ ____ becoming a nurse, she should become a mother and stay home with the

children. She has so much homework that she ____ has time to cook and clean properly. They

_____ much of the time, and he has begun _____ ____ of the house and coming home late, his

breath smelling of alcohol. She still loves him and he loves her, but she must make a decision:

_____ or stay married.

Housing discrimination: move or stay?

DECISION DRAMA 11

PREVIEW

What do you know about housing discrimination and racism? Have you ever experienced housing discrimination of any sort? What can be done about this serious problem?

KEY VOCABULARY

electrical engineer, subject to, harassment, threatening, KKK, fearful, withdrawn, cope, dental technician, discrimination, protection, intimidation, promotion, incidents, neighborhood, die down.

BACKGROUND INFORMATION

Jorge is a 36 year old Hispanic with a wife and three children. He is an electrical engineer and has recently been promoted. Three months ago he moved his family into an all white Anglo neighborhood. From the day he moved in, he and his family have been subject to harassment. They get threatening phone calls and letters. Their children are called bad names and threatened also. Recently, they were sent a dead animal in the mail, and the letters KKK were written on their door. The children are beginning to be afraid to go out and play after school. In school they are shy, fearful and withdrawn. Jorge's wife is also finding it hard to cope and is thinking of giving up her job as a dental technician to be with the children. Jorge, however, does not want to give in to intimidation and discrimination and has reported the incidents to the police. The police say they will help but cannot promise him 24 hour protection. He must decide soon what he wants to do: wait to be accepted by the community or leave.

POSSIBLE ROLES

Jorge, wife, children, friends, family members, the police.

THE DECISION

Predicted Decision _____

Decision Reached _____

Reason for Decision _____

Exercises

Exercise I: Follow up assignment

Choose one of the following.

1. Write a composition on discrimination in housing. What examples of this do you know about?

2. Write a letter from Jorge to the people he believes are harassing him and his family.

3. Write a conversation that the family has about whether to stay or move.

Exercise II: Conversation Practice

In groups of two or more fill in and practice the following conversation. Use the vocabulary from the Key Vocabulary section.

X: Hello, Jorge. How are you? We haven't heard from you recently.

Y: Well, things here haven't been too good.

X: What's wrong?

Y: You know, I recently got a _____ so I moved the family into an all Anglo _____. I thought the schools would be better for the kids. But from the day we moved in we have experienced all kinds of _____.

X: But you're a professional. You're an _____!

Y: That doesn't seem to matter to these people. Every day or so we get _____ phone calls and letters. The kids have been called bad names and threatened.

X: That's terrible! Things like that never happened at home. Is there more?

Y: Yes, unfortunately there's more. Just recently someone sent a _____ animal in the mail and the letters _____ were written on our door!

X: How're your wife and children taking it.

Y: The kids are starting to be shy, _____ and _____. My wife is finding it hard to _____ with the situation. She is thinking of giving up her job as a _____ to be with the kids more.

X: Have you notified the police?

Y: Yes, we've reported the incidents. But they say they can't promise me 24 hour _____. At the beginning I thought that these incidents would soon die down, but now I'm not so sure.

X: Why don't you just move out?

Y: I don't want to give in to _____ and _____. Besides I have an investment in this house and I don't want to lose it. I just don't know what to do next.

X: Well, if there's any way I can help, please let me know.

Exercise III: Vocabulary Practice

Fill in the blanks with the appropriate words.

Jorge is a 36 year old _____ with a _____ and three children. He is an electrical _____ and has recently been promoted. Three months _____ he moved his family into an all Anglo _____. From the day he moved in, he and his family have been _____ ___ harrassment. They get _____ phone calls and letters. Their children are called bad names and _____ also. Recently, they were sent a _____ animal in the mail, and the letters KKK were written on their door. The children are beginning to be afraid to go _____ and play after school. In school they are shy, fearful and _____. Jorge's wife is also _____ it hard to cope and is _____ of giving up her job as a _____ technician to be with the children. Jorge, however, does not want to give in to _____ and_____ and has reported the _____ to the police. The police say that they will help but cannot _____ him 24 hour protection. He must decide _____ what he wants to do: wait to be accepted by the _____ or leave.

8
/th/   tings

Date an American or not?

DECISION DRAMA 12

PREVIEW

How do you feel about dating someone who is not from your native country? How do your parents feel about it? Have you ever dated an American? How is dating an American different from dating someone from your native country?

KEY VOCABULARY

immigrant, go out, customs, Americanize, respect, too fast, sufficiently, shy, point of view, disobey

BACKGROUND INFORMATION

Sara is an immigrant who has been in the United States for two years. She is sixteen and a junior in high school. Last night an American boy from her social studies class asked her to go out with him. Her English is still not too good and she is shy, but she likes this boy. The problem is with her parents. They don't want her to go out with an American boy. They say he has different customs and ways of thinking. They don't want their daughter to Americanize because they plan to return to their native country one day. In addition, some of their friends' daughters have had bad experiences dating Americans. They say American boys are too fast and don't respect their daughters sufficiently.

Sara understands her parents' point of view and wants to please them. On the other hand, she likes the American boy and thinks he is "different" from the average American. Now she must decide whether or not to disobey her parents and go out with him.

POSSIBLE ROLES

Sara, parents, brothers, sister, friends (American and non-American), boyfriend.

THE DECISION

Predicted Decision _____

Decision Reached _____

Reason for Decision _____

Exercises

Exercise I: Follow up assignment

Choose one of the following.

1. Write about an experience you or someone you know had dating someone from another country or culture.

2. Do you agree or disagree with Sara's decision? Tell why.

3. Compare and contrast dating in the United States with dating in your native country.

Exercise II: Conversation Practice

In groups of two or more fill in and practice the following conversation.

X: I've got to talk to you. I have a big problem.

Y: What happened?

X: Last night an _____ boy from my _____ class asked me to _____ with him.

Y: Do you like him?

X: Yes, I think he's nice.

Y: So what's the problem?

X: The problem is with my _____. They are old-fashioned and won't let me _____ _____ with an American boy. They say he has different _____ and ways of thinking. Besides, they don't want me to _____ because they are thinking of going back to our native country one day. In addition, they say some of their friends' daughters have had bad experiences _____ Americans. They are too _____ and don't _____ their daughters _____.

Y: What are you going to do?

X: I don't really know. But I know this. I like this boy. He's _____ from the _____ American. But I'm still a little _____ and my English is not so good. What should I do?

Y: It's a hard decision. Do what you think is best.

Exercise III: Vocabulary Practice

Fill in the blanks with the appropriate words.

      Sara is an _____ who has been in the United States for two years. She is sixteen and a junior in high school. Last night an American boy from her _____ _____ class asked her to go out with him. Her English is _____ not too good and she is _____, but she likes this _____. The problem is with her parents. They don't want to _____ her to go out with an American boy. They say he has different _____ and ways of _____. They don't want their daughter to Americanize because they _____ to return one day to their native country. In addition, some of their friends' daughters have had bad _____ dating Americans. Now Sara has to decide whether or not to _____ her parents and go out with him.

Who will take care of the baby?

DECISION DRAMA 13

PREVIEW

What do you feel about child care in this country? If you have children, who takes care of them while you are in school? If you have no children at present, who would you like to take care of your future children while you work or study?

KEY VOCABULARY

Radiology, pursue, career, inadequate, day care, heart condition, private, opposite, expensive, limited, native language, day care center.

BACKGROUND INFORMATION

Mary has a 2½ year old child and is planning to return to college to pursue her degree in radiology. She has a serious problem. She must decide who will take care of the baby and whether she should attend school at night or in regular session. Her husband works all day. When he comes home he is usually tired and needs her attention. He is willing to take care of the child a few nights a week because he doesn't want the child to go to an inadequate day-care center. On the other hand, he is usually too tired to play with the child, and often watches television at night. Also, if Mary goes to school at night it might take four years to complete a two year program.

Mary's mother lives nearby. If she goes to school during the day Mary can leave her child with her mother. However, her mother is over sixty-five and has a heart condition. In addition, her mother speaks only their native language and cannot speak English. Mary's child doesn't talk much yet, but she wants her child to learn English quickly.

The school Mary is going to has a day-care center which is free and fairly good, but only has limited hours to offer. She would have no free-time to study. Also, the majority of children speak her child's native language. There is another private day-care center nearby, but it is more expensive and in the opposite direction from her school. She would have to leave the child there very early in the morning to get to school on time. However, its program is good and her child could learn English there. The decision has to be made soon because school is starting in a few weeks.

POSSIBLE ROLES

Mary, mother, father, husband, other student-mother, friend, director of school day care center, director of private day care center, a teacher advisor etc.

THE DECISION

Predicted Decision _____

Decision Reached _____

Reason for Decision _____

Exercises

Exercise I: Follow up assignment

Choose one of the following and write a short composition.

1. Write a persuasive letter from one of the directors of the day care centers to Mary describing the advantages of its program.

2. Compare day care in your native country with day care in the United States. Which system is better and why?

3. Is day care good for children? Why or why not?

Exercise II: Conversation Practice

In groups of two or more fill in and practice the following conversation. Use the vocabulary from the Key Vocabulary section.

X: I don't know what to do. I want to _____ a degree in _____ but don't know where I should leave my child.

Y: What about your husband?

X: He works hard and is tired at night. He says he'll take care of the child a few nights a week because he doesn't want the child in an _____ day care center.

Y: Is he supportive of your _____?

X: Yes, but he wants me to put him and the child first.

Y: What about your mother?

X: She wants to help me, but she is over sixty-five and she has a _____ _____.

Y: What about the school _____ _____ center?

X: It's free and it's fairly good, but it has only _____ hours to offer. In addition, all the students speak my child's _____. I would prefer that she learn English.

Y: What about a _____ day care center?

X: There is a good one near here but it is more _____ and is in the _____ direction from my school. The program is good and my child could learn English there, but could we afford it?

Y: I don't know what to tell you. You'll have to make a decision soon. Call me and let me know what you decide.

Exercise III: Vocabulary Practice

Fill in the blanks with the appropriate words.

Mary has a 2¹/2 year old child and is _____ to return to college to _____ her _____ in radiology. She has a _____ problem. She must decide who will take care of the _____ and whether she should _____ school at night or in regular _____. Her husband _____ all day. When he _____ home he is usually _____ and needs her _____. He is willing to _____ care of the child a few _____ a _____ because he _____ want the child to go to an _____ day care center. On the other hand, he is _____ too tired to ____ with the child, and often _____ television at night. Also, if Mary goes to school at night it _____ take four years to _____ a two year program.

Mary's mother lives _____. If she goes to school _____ the day, Mary can _____ her child with her _____. However, her mother is _____ sixty-five and has a _____ condition. In addition, her mother ____ only their native language and _____ speak English. Mary's child doesn't _____ much yet, but she wants her child to _____ English _____.

The _____ Mary is going to has a _____ _____ center which is free and ____ good, but only has _____ hours to offer. Mary _____ have no free time to _____. Also, the _____ of children speak her child's _____ language. There is another _____ day care center nearby, but it is more _____ and in the opposite _____ from her school. She would have to _____ the child there very _____ in the morning to get to school _____ time. However, its _____ is good and her child could _____ English there. The _____ has to be made soon because _____ is starting in a _____ weeks.

AIDS and the schools: Send your child to school or not?

PREVIEW

What do you know about AIDS? How is it transmitted? Do you know anyone who has AIDS? Would you send your child to school if he had AIDS? Would you send your child to school where another child has AIDS?

KEY VOCABULARY

positive, hemophiliac, concerned, worried, blood transfusion, reassured, skeptical, virus, protest, legal, transmitted, insults, cruelty, tutor.

BACKGROUND INFORMATION

Linda is the mother of a fourth grader. Recently her son, who is a hemophiliac, tested HIV positive for AIDS as a result of a blood transfusion. Most of the parents of the children in that elementary school are very concerned and worried. Although experts have reassured the parents that their children aren't in any danger, some remain skeptical. They feel that no one really knows for sure how AIDS is transmitted. They fear that their children may somehow be exposed to this deadly virus through contact with the infected child. Some of them have even decided to keep their children at home in protest.

Linda's son is not ill at this time. Although he has a legal right to go to public school Linda is afraid that he would be exposed to other children's cruelty and insults. Perhaps it would be better if she kept him home and got a tutor. On the other hand, he loves school and his friends and would be terribly sad and lonely at home alone.

School begins tomorrow and Linda must make a decision as to whether she will send her child back to school or keep him home.

POSSIBLE ROLES

Linda, husband, fourth grader, another parent of an HIV positive child, parents who have decided to keep their children home, parents who intend to send their children to school, an AIDS expert, principal of the school, friends, relatives.

THE DECISION

Predicted Decision _____

Decision Reached _____

Reason for Decision _____

Exercises

Exercise I: Follow up assignment

Choose one of the following and write a short editorial or composition.

1. What do you think should be done to stop the spread of AIDS?

2. Write a newspaper editorial in support of or against allowing an AIDS infected child to attend school.

3. Write about someone you know who has AIDS or has died of AIDS.

Exercise II: Conversation Practice

In groups of two or more fill in and practice the following conversation. Use the vocabulary from the Key Vocabulary section.

X: I'm so upset I just don't know what to do.

Y: What's the problem?

X: My son is a _____. He recently tested HIV _____ as a result of a _____ _____. Now I don't know whether to send him to school or not.

Y: What's the problem with sending him to school?

X: Some parents are very _____ and _____. Although experts have _____ them that their children aren't in any danger, they are still _____. They feel that no one really knows for sure how AIDS is _____. They fear their children might be exposed to this deadly _____ by contact with my child. Some of them are even keeping their children at home in _____.

Y: That's very upsetting. What are you going to do?

X: I don't know. My son is not ill now and he has a _____ right to go to public school, but I'm afraid to expose him to the possible _____ and _____ of other children. Maybe I should just keep him home and get a _____.

Y: Won't he be lonely by himself all the time?

X: He might be. He loves his school and his friends. I just don't know what to do.

Exercise III: Vocabulary Practice

Fill in the blanks with the appropriate words.

Linda is the mother of a _____ grader. Recently, her son _____ is a _____ has tested HIV

_____ for AIDS as a result of a _____ transfusion. Most of the _____ of the children in that

_____school are very _____ and worried. Although _____ have _____ the parents that their

_____ aren't in any _____, some remain _____. They feel that no one _____ knows for

sure how AIDS is _____. They fear that their children _____ somehow be _____ to this deadly

_____ through contact with the _____ child. Some of them have even _____ to keep their

children _____ home in _____.

Linda's son is not _____ at this time. Although he has a _____ right to go to _____

school, Linda is _____ that he would be _____ to other children's _____ and _____.

Perhaps it would be better if she _____ him home and got a _____. On the other hand, he

_____ school and his friends and would be _____ sad and _____ at home _____.

School _____ tomorrow and Linda must make a _____ as to _____ she will _____ her

_____ back to school or _____ him home.

Work or go to summer school?

DECISION DRAMA 15

PREVIEW

Have you ever gone to high school summer school? Did you like it? Why or why not. If you failed a subject would you make it up in summer school? Have you ever worked during the summer? Did you enjoy it?

KEY VOCABULARY

sophomore, advanced, failed, accepted, acceptance, make up a subject.

BACKGROUND INFORMATION

Martin is generally a good student but failed math last semester. He is in his sophomore year in high school, so next year these grades will be sent to college. He is thinking of making up the math class in summer school so he can take a more advanced math course he will need in the fall. However, he wants money to buy clothes and certain other things he needs for the next school year. He also wants to help his parents, who don't have much money.

Martin would like a break from school, but he knows that making up the failed subject is important. It could help him get acceptance to the college of his choice. Martin must make a decision soon.

POSSIBLE ROLES

Martin, parents, other family members, fellow students, friends, boyfriend/girlfriend, college counselor, job placement counselor.

THE DECISION

Predicted Decision _Summers_ _Math_

Decision Reached _____

Reason for Decision _____

Exercises

Exercise I: Follow up assignment

Choose one of the following.

1. What are the advantages and disadvantages of going to summer school? Have you ever gone? How did you like it?

2. Tell about an experience you had working during the summer.

3. Write Martin a letter in which you agree or disagree with his decision.

Exercise II: Conversation Practice

In groups of two or more fill in and practice the following conversation. Use the vocabulary words from the Key Vocabulary section.

X: I'm not sure whether to go to ____ _____ or get a job. If I go to school I can _____ _____ the math course I failed and take a more _____ math course that I'll need next semester. On the other hand, if I get a job, I'll be able to help my _____. I could also use the money to buy _____ and other things for the following year.

Y: That sounds like a good idea. Why don't you do that?

X: Because I need a good grade to get into to the college of my choice.

Y: Well, it's your life. I hope you make the right decision.

Exercise III: Vocabulary Practice

Fill in the blanks with the appropriate word.

Martin is generally a good student but failed math last _____. As he is in his _____ year in high school, next year these grades will be sent to _____. He is thinking of taking math in _____ school so he can take a more _____ math course he will need in the fall. However, he wants money to buy clothes and certain other things he needs for the next school year. He also wants to help his _____ who don't have much money.

Martin would like a _____ from school, but knows that ____ _____ the _____ subject is important. It could help him get _____ to the college of his choice. Martin must make a decision soon.

Harvard or the University of Miami?

DECISION DRAMA 16

PREVIEW

Where would you like to go to college if you had the choice? What would most influence your choice: location, cost, reputation of the institution, the quality of instruction etc?

KEY VOCABULARY

prestigious, partial, environmental science, powerful, approximately, ecology, open doors, repay, resembles, climate.

BACKGROUND INFORMATION

John is a foreign student in the United States who has a serious problem. He has been accepted to two colleges and must make a choice by the end of May where to study ecology and environmental science.

The first school which accepted him is Harvard University in Cambridge, Massachusetts. The other is the University of Miami in Florida. Harvard is, of course, a highly prestigious Ivy League University. The richest and most powerful people in the United States and the world send their sons and daughters to Harvard. John has always dreamed of attending Harvard. In fact, a Harvard degree might open doors that otherwise would be shut. However, he has received only a partial scholarship. It will cover most of his tuition and room and board, but he will still have to borrow approximately $2,500 a year. Thus, when John graduates from Harvard he will have a debt of over $10,000 to repay. As his family is not rich, he cannot count on his parents to help repay the loan.

On the other hand, the University of Miami, which has an excellent ecology department, has offered John a full four-year scholarship, so he would have no debt to repay at the end of the four years. In addition, the climate in Miami closely resembles the climate in his native country. However, this university is unknown in John's native country.

A decision must be made in the next few weeks. What will he do?

POSSIBLE ROLES   John, parents, friends, relatives, teachers, college advisors, girlfriend, etc.

THE DECISION   Predicted Decision _____

Decision Reached _____

Reason For Decision _____

Exercises

Exercise I: Follow up assignment

Choose one of the following and write a composition.

1. What are the advantages and disadvantages of going to an Ivy League School?

2. Write a paragraph explaining why you chose to go to the school you are now attending. How does it compare to other schools you have attended?

3. Pretend you are John and it is a year later. Write why you think you made a good or bad decision.

Exercise II: Conversation Practice

In groups of two or more fill in and practice the following conversation. Use the vocabulary from the Key Vocabulary Words.

X: I don't know which university to choose, Harvard or the University of Miami?

Y: Which one is more _____?

X: Harvard is much more famous and well-regarded, but it's also very expensive.

Y: How much is it?

X: The _____ is over $15,000 a year. I am getting a _____ scholarship, but I would have to borrow _____ $2,500 annually. When I graduate I will have to _____ about $10,000.

Y: What about the University of Miami?

X: It has an excellent _____ department and the _____ in Miami _____ my native country. In addition, they have offered me a full four year scholarship so I'd have no _____ to repay.

Y: Well, that's a tough decision. I wouldn't want to be in your shoes! Good luck!

Exercise III: Vocabulary Practice

Fill in the blanks with the appropriate words.

John is a foreign _____ in the United States who has a serious problem. John has been

_____ to two _____ and must make a _____ by the end of May where to study _____

and _____ science.

The first school which _____ John was Harvard University at Cambridge, Massachusetts.

The other was the University of Miami in _____. Harvard is, of course, a highly _____ Ivy

League University. The _____ and most _____ people in the United States and the world send

their sons and daughters to Harvard. John has always dreamed of _____ Harvard. In fact, a

Harvard _____ might open doors that otherwise _____ be shut.

However, John has _____ only a _____ scholarship. It would cover most of his ____ and

_____, but John will still have to _____ approximately $2,500 a year. Thus, when John _____

from Harvard he will have a _____ of over $10,000 to _____. As his family is not _____,

he can't _____ on his parents to help repay the _____.

On the other hand, the University of Miami, which has an excellent _____ department,

has _____ John a full four-year ____, so he will have no _____ to repay at the _____ of the

four _____. In addition, the climate in Miami closely _____ the climate in his _____

country. However, this university is _____ in his native _____.

Mixed marriage: Marry or not?

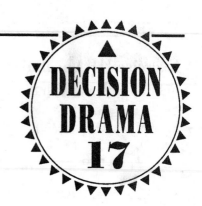

DECISION DRAMA 17

PREVIEW

How do you feel about inter-racial, inter-religious marriage? Do you think it works? What problems arise? Would you consider marriage with someone outside of your race or religion? Why or why not? What effect does it have on children?

KEY VOCABULARY

religious, close, Jewish, Catholic, orthodox, resident, medicine, in common, insists, tradition, background, single.

BACKGROUND INFORMATION

David comes from a close, highly religious Catholic family from the Caribbean. He is completing his studies in medicine. He has met a lovely American girl who is a resident at his hospital. They have a lot in common except that she is Jewish. She, too, comes from a religious home. Her parents are orthodox and want her to marry someone of her own background. His parents are anxious for their son to marry someone from their native country, or at least someone Catholic. David and his girlfriend are very much in love and agree on most things. However, they have a problem when it comes to deciding which religion their children will be. David would like them to be Catholic, while his girlfriend insists they learn and practice Jewish traditions. David must make a decision: whether or not to marry his Jewish girlfriend.

POSSIBLE ROLES

David, Jewish girlfriend, his family, her family, friends, a priest, a rabbi.

THE DECISION

Predicted Decision _____

Decision Reached _____

Reason for Decision _____

Exercises

Exercise I

Choose one of the following.

1. Write a conversation between David and his parents about his possible marriage to his Jewish girlfriend.

2. Do you think this kind of inter-racial or inter-religious marriage is a good idea? Why or why not?

3. Write about an experience you have had or have heard about involving an inter-racial or inter-religious marriage.

Exercise II: Conversation Practice

In groups of two or more fill in and practice the following conversation. Use the vocabulary from the Key Vocabulary section.

X: I hear you're getting married. Congratulations!

Y: Thanks, but I'm not completely sure I'm going to go through with it.

X: What's the problem?

Y: Well, we have a lot in common. Both of us are studying _____. In fact, she is a _____ in the hospital where I work. However, I come from a close, highly _____ Catholic family and she is from a _____ American family who are also religious. In fact, she is from an _____ family and they want her to marry someone from her own _____.

X: I don't think it will be a big problem. Recent statistics show that about 52% of American Jews intermarry. And in your native country there is also inter-marriage among different racial groups.

Y: Yes, but the problem is really how to raise the children. She wants them to learn and practice Jewish _____. But, I would like them to be _____.

X: Maybe they could be taught both religions.

Y: You're right. But I'm beginning to have second thoughts. Should I marry and face all these problems or should I not?

X: I guess that's for you to decide.

Exercise III: Vocabulary Practice

Fill in the blanks with the appropriate words.

   David comes from a close, highly _____ Catholic family from the Carribean. He is completing

his studies in _____ and has met a lovely American girl who is a resident at his _____. They have

a lot _____ _____ except that she is Jewish. She also comes from a _____ home. Her parents are

_____ and want her to marry someone of her own _____. His parents are anxious for their son to

_____ someone form their native _____ or at least someone _____. David and his girlfriend

are very much in love and agree on most things. However, they have a problem when it comes to

deciding which religion their _____ will be. David would like them to be _____, while his girlfriend

insists that they learn and practice Jewish _____. David must make a _____: marry his Jewish

girlfriend or not.

More money or more time?

DECISION DRAMA 18

PREVIEW

What are your reasons for choosing the career you are presently pursuing? What factors entered into the decision? Are you thinking of changing your career? Why?

KEY VOCABULARY

factors, single parent, related, majoring in, schedule, devote, considering, provide, path, computer programming, private industry.

BACKGROUND INFORMATION

Carol is a single parent who has just completed two years of college. Because she has done very well in her math courses, she has decided to find work related to math. On one hand, she is thinking of majoring in education and becoming a math teacher. She enjoys teaching very much, as she likes to see people grow and develop. She also would be on a school schedule, and would be able to devote more time to her child. On the other hand, she is considering majoring in computer programming. She has taken courses which indicate that she would do well in this field. She would be able to get a higher paying job and provide a better future for both of them. But in private industry the hours are long and vacations are short. Much of the extra income she would take home would go toward child care. Registration is next week and she must decide what path to take.

POSSIBLE ROLES

Carol, math teacher, computer programmer, school advisor, parents, friends, etc.

THE DECISION   Predicted Decision _____

Decision Reached _____

Reason for Decision _____

Exercises

Exercise I: Follow up assignment

Choose one of the following.

1. Write a paragraph in which you explain why you would or would not like to become a teacher. Be specific.

2. Write a paragraph telling why you think Carol's decision was a good or bad one for her and her child.

3. Explain the reasons why you chose the career you did. Be specific.

Exercise II: Conversation Practice

In groups of two or more fill in and practice the following conversation. Use the vocabulary from the Key Vocabulary section.

X: How can I help you?

Y: I need some advice. I have just completed two years of college. I do very well in math and I'm thinking of a career _____ to math.

X: There are many paths you could follow. You could work in private industry or with computer companies. There are many opportunities open to you.

Y: Yes, but I've been thinking of _____ education and teaching math. You see, I have a child and I'm a _____ _____. I like teaching and I would also have the same _____ as my child. I would be able to _____ more time to her. On the other hand, I'm also _____ majoring in _____.

X: Yes, you could make more money and _____ a better future for your child if you did this.

Y: Well, registration is next week and I still don't know which _____ to take.

X: The only thing I can advise you to do is think about it. Only you know what is best for you.

Exercise III: Vocabulary Practice

Fill in the blanks with the appropriate words.

Carol is a single _____ who has just completed two _____ of college. Because she has done very well in her math _____, she has decided to do something _____ to math. On one hand, she is thinking of _____ in education and _____ a math teacher. She _____ teaching very much and she likes to see people _____ and develop. She also would be on a school _____, and would be able to _____ more time to her child.

On the other hand, she is _____ majoring in computer programming. She has taken courses that _____ that she would do well in this _____. She _____ be able to get a higher paying job and _____ a better _____ for both of them. But in private industry, the hours are _____ and vacations are _____. Much of the _____ income she would take _____ would go toward child care. _____ is next week and she must decide what _____ to take.

Have an abortion or have the baby?

DECISION DRAMA 19

PREVIEW

How do you feel about abortion? Should a woman have a right to choose whether to have an abortion or not? Under what conditions, if any, do you think abortion is justified? What are the psychological effects of abortion on women?

KEY VOCABULARY

abortion, laid off, supporting, accounting, qualified, intends, nursing program, goal, frustrated, secure, rewarding, relationship, strained, pregnant, intensive, professionals, argue, concern, counted on, breaking point.

BACKGROUND INFORMATION

Malia was a full-time student. Her husband worked, and was a part-time student. He was laid off from his job recently. Now she is supporting them by working full-time in an office while he goes to school full-time to complete his program in accounting. She is only able to go to school two nights a week. When she is qualified, Malia intends to study nursing. This is a very demanding program which requires at least two years of intensive work. However, it will lead to a secure and rewarding job in the future. Since her husband lost his job, their relationship has become strained. He doesn't like to feel he is not supporting the family. They argue about money and feel generally frustrated. They each came to this country to become professionals. This has been their main goal.

Now Malia has discovered that she is six weeks pregnant. She and her husband had talked and looked forward to having children, but always many years in the future. All of her family and most of his live in their native countries. They could not be counted on either for financial support or to help take care of the baby. Malia isn't sure she wants to tell her husband she is pregnant.

Malia is considering getting an abortion. She thinks her husband would be completely opposed to this, however, and it concerns her very much. If Malia decides to have the baby, it will be a great financial problem and will certainly destroy her career plans. On the other hand, she fears an abortion could strain their marriage to the breaking point. A decision has to be made soon.

POSSIBLE ROLES Malia, co-workers, friends, family members, college advisor, nursing program advisor.

THE DECISION Predicted Decision _____

Decision Reached _____

Reason for Decision _____

Exercises

Exercise I: Follow up assignment

Choose one of the following.

1. Write a conversation between Malia and her husband about the pregnancy and the possible abortion.

2. Write a composition for or against abortion. Give your reasons.

3. What is the current status of abortion in the United States? What are various groups doing to change this?

Exercise II: Conversation Practice

In groups of two or more fill in the blanks and practice the following conversation. Use the vocabulary words from the Key Vocabulary section.

X: What's the matter? You don't look very happy today.

Y: I just found out that I'm 6 weeks _____ and I don't know what to do.

X: Have you told your husband?

Y: Not yet. He's part of the problem.

X: What's the problem with him?

Y: He was _____ _____ from his job a while ago and can't find another one, so he's gone back to school to finish a program in _____. I'm _____ him now by working full-time in an office.

X: I thought you were going to school full-time.

Y: I used to, but now I go to school at night to be _____ to study nursing.

X: What about the future?

Y: Well, I intended to enter a _____ _____. It's a _____ program that requires at least two years of _____ work but it would mean a _____ and _____ job in the future. Now I don't know what the future holds.

X: Do you want to have children?

Y: We talked of having children but it was always way in the future when we could afford them. We both want to become _____. Recently with all our economic problems we _____ with each other and feel _____.

X: What about your family? Could they help you?

Y: Not really. All of my family and most of his live in our native countries. Nobody could really help us take care of the baby. Now I have to decide whether to have the baby or have an abortion.

X: Well, you have a tough decision to make.

Exercise III: Vocabulary Practice

Fill in the blanks with the appropriate words.

Malia used to be a full-time student until her husband was ____ ___ from his job. Now she is _____ him by working _____ in an office, while he goes back to school to _____ a program in _____. In addition, she is going to school two nights a week. When she is _____ she _____ to study nursing. This is a very _____ program which _____ at least two years of _____ work. However, it will ____ ____ a secure and rewarding _____ in the future. Since her husband lost his job, their _____ has become _____. He doesn't like to feel he is not _____ the family. They argue about money and feel generally _____. They each came to this country to become _____. This has been their main _____.

Now Malia has discovered that she is 6 weeks _____. She and her husband had talked of having _____, but always many years in the _____. All of her _____ and most of his live in their native countries. They could not be _____ _____ to help take care of the baby.

If Malia decides to have the baby it will certainly destroy her _____ plans. On the other hand, she fears an abortion could strain their marriage to the _____ _____. A decision has to be made soon.

Job discrimination: quit or fight?

DECISION
DRAMA
20

PREVIEW

What do you know about job discrimination? Have you or anyone you know been a victim of job discrimination? Do you know about equal opportunity laws?

KEY VOCABULARY

minority, degree, accountant, available, prestigious, supervisor, discriminated against, effectively, compensation, suffered, risk, trouble-maker, hire, reference, promotion, file a charge, in a bind.

BACKGROUND INFORMATION

Anna is a twenty-six year old minority woman. After getting her degree in accounting, she went to work for a large company. She has been working there as a junior accountant for four years. Recently, a higher position became available. Anna was interviewed for the position but it was given to a white man who had just gotten his degree. He had gone to a more prestigious college than Anna, but she feels she has more experience and direct knowledge of the job. She finds it even more difficult because he will be her immediate supervisor. She is hurt and angry and feels discriminated against. She thinks that these feelings might prevent her from working effectively in the company. She has to make a decision. She can keep her feelings to herself and stay on the job, hoping to get a promotion in the future. She can remain and file discrimination charges. She can leave the company without complaint and get a good letter of recommendation for her next job. She can leave and then file a discrimination charge against the company, asking for compensation for the discrimination she suffered. The risk is that if she doesn't win she might be seen as a "trouble-maker" and would not get a good letter of reference from her employers. Other employers might also see her as a trouble-maker and not hire her. The decision must be made soon.

POSSIBLE ROLES   Anna, family members, boyfriend, co-workers, a lawyer, a representative of the Equal Opportunity Commission.

THE DECISION   Predicted Decision Andrew—stay + complaint

Decision Reached _____

Reason for Decision _____

Exercises

Exercise I: Follow up assignment

Choose one of the following.

1. Write a letter of resignation from the company you work for, in which you politely, but firmly charge them with discrimination.

2. Write a story about discrimination in school, jobs, housing etc.

3. Research the equal opportunity laws and give a report on how they are usually enforced.

Exercise II: Conversation Practice

In groups of two or more fill in and practice the following conversation. Use the vocabulary from the Key Vocabulary section.

X: I've got a difficult decision to make and I'd like your advice.

Y: Sure, tell me what's going on.

X: Well, you know how hard it is for a _____ woman to make it in the business world. There's so much discrimination. My case is that after getting my _____ in accounting, I joined a large company. I've been working in this company as a junior _____ for four years. However, when a higher position became _____ it went to a white man who had just gotten a degree from a _____ college.

Y: The same old story. Well, can you live with it?

X: I don't think I can. He is going to be my _____! I feel so _____. I'm thinking of leaving and filing a discrimination charge against the company.

Y: Well, why don't you do it?

X: If I lose I won't be able to get a good letter of _____ and other employers might see me as a _____ and they might not _____ me.

Y: Why don't you just leave the company without complaint then.

X: After all, I have _____ and direct knowledge. I don't know if I could do that.

Y: Well, then stay where you are hope the next time they'll give you a _____.

X: Thanks, but I'm not sure I could work there _____ anymore.

Y: You're really in a bind. I hope for your sake that you make the right decision.

Exercise III: Vocabulary Practice

Fill in the blanks with the appropriate words.

Anna is a twenty-six year old _____ woman. After getting her degree in accounting, she went to work for a large _____. She has been _____ there as a junior _____ for four years. Recently, a higher position became _____. Anna was _____ for the position, but it was given to a _____ man who had just gotten his _____. He had gone to a more _____ college than Anna, but she feels she has more _____ and direct knowledge about the job. She _____ it even more difficult because he will be her _____ supervisor. She is hurt and _____ and feels discriminated _____. She thinks that these _____ might _____ her from working _____ in the company. She has to make a decision. She can keep her feelings to _____ and stay on the job, hoping to get a _____ in the future. She can remain and file _____ charges. She can leave the company _____ complaint and get a _____ letter of _____ for her next job. She can leave and then file a discrimination _____ against the company asking for _____ for the discrimination she _____. The risk is that if she doesn't win she might be fired as a "_____ _____" and would not get a good _____ of reference from her _____. Other employers might see her as a trouble-maker and not _____ her.

Appendix: Useful Expressions for Decision Dramas

Giving Suggestions

Here are some ways to give suggestions.

1. I suggest that...
2. I recommend that...
3. Don't you think that...
4. Wouldn't it be better if...
5. Wouldn't it be a good idea to...
6. I advise that...
7. Perhaps you could...
8. Why don't you...
9. How about...
10. Why not...
11. If I were you, I'd...
12. You'd better...
13. If I were in your place, I'd...
14. If I were in your shoes I'd...

Accepting Suggestions

You can accept suggestions to varying degrees. Here are some expressions that reflect varying degrees of acceptance.

Strong Acceptance

1. That sounds like a great idea.
2. Yes, I agree with that.
3. I think you're right.
4. I think you've got something there.
5. Yes, why don't I?

Hesitant Acceptance

1. Perhaps you're right.
2. Maybe I should try that.
3. Maybe I'll do that.
4. That sounds like it might work out.
5. You might be right about that.

Rejected Suggestions
Suggestions can be rejected in various ways:

Strong Rejection

1. No, I don't want to do that.
2. I don't agree with you.
3. No, that's no good.
4. No, that wouldn't work.
5. I don't see any advantage in doing that.

Mild Rejection

1. That doesn't sound too good.
2. I'm not sure that would work.
3. I don't think I would do that.
4. Is there anything else you would suggest?
5. That's not exactly what I want.
6. What else would you do in my position?

Expressing agreement or disagreement
These words can be used to express agreement or disagreement in a conversation.

Agreement	Disagreement
1. Yes.	1. No way
2. Yeah.	2. Impossible!
3. O.K..	3. Ridiculous!
4. Right.	4. Oh, come on.
5. I see.	5. Uh Uh.
6. Sure.	6. Definitely not.
7. I know.	7. Forget it.
8. Exactly.	8. No chance.
9. I agree.	

10. Of course.
11. Naturally.
12. Definitely.
13. Great!
14. Terrific!
15. Fantastic!
16. Marvellous!
17. You bet!
18. Awesome.
19. Right on!

Doubt

1. Maybe…
2. Perhaps
3. Well…
4. Oh, really?
5. Possibly.

Thanking
When people give you suggestions you may thank them for their help.

1. Thanks a million, a lot, so much.
2. You've really been a great help.
3. Thanks for your advice.
4. I really appreciate your help.
5. What a help you've been!
6. How can I thank you enough?
7. Thanks for your time.
8. Thanks for everything.

Responding to Thanks

1. You're very welcome.
2. No trouble at all.
3. I'm happy to be of help.
4. It's really been good talking to you.
5. Let me know how things work out.

6. Let me know if I can be of any more help.

7. Glad I could help.

8. Keep in touch.

9. It was my pleasure.

Paraphrasing

When you want to restate in your own words what the speaker has just said, or tell something again in other words.

1. What you're saying is that...

2. If I understand you correctly...

3. What you're trying to say is that...

4. In other words...

5. What you mean to say is that...

6. Do you mean...

7. I'm trying to tell you that...

8. I'd like to say that...

9. What I'm trying to tell you is...

10. I really want to tell you that...

11. I mean that...

12. To put it another way...

References

Di Pietro, R. (1982). The open-ended scenario: A new approach to conversation. *TESOL Quarterly*, 16, 15-20.

Maley, A., and Duff, A. (1982). *Drama Techniques in Language Learning*. Cambridge University Press.

Radin, B. (1987). The Effects of Two Communicative Approaches on the Communicative Competence of Adult Hispanic College ESL Students. Unpublished Doctoral Dissertation. Fordham University.

Stern, S. (1983). Why drama works: A psycholinguistic perspective. *Language Learning*, 30, 77-97.

Spolin, V. (1963). *Improvisation for the theater*. Evanston, Ill.: Northwestern University Press.

ABOUT THE AUTHOR Dr. Barbara Radin has been teaching at Hostos Community College since 1981, specializing in ESL and English through drama. This is her first published work.

OTHER BOOKS AVAILABLE FROM JAG PUBLICATIONS:

Comics and Conversation

More Comics and Conversation

Foreign Students' Guide to Pronunciation

Begin In English, Volume 1

Begin In English, Volume 2

Motivational Strategies: Text and Transparencies in Composition and Grammar

From the Beginning: A First Reader in American History

Rhythm and Role Play